HARRY H

A Life from Beginning to End

Table of Contents

Introduction

Harry Houdini made his first debut on March 24, 1874, when he was born to a Jewish scholar and rabbi by the name of Mayer Samuel Weisz and his wife, Cecilia. Cecilia was Mayer's second wife, as his first wife had perished while giving birth to Harry's older brother Herman. In all, the Weisz children consisted of Herman, Nathan, Gottfried, Theodore, Leopold, Carrie, and of course, Harry Houdini.

It must be mentioned that Harry's birth name was not Harry but rather Erik, and as you might have guessed, his last name wasn't Houdini either but rather the family name of Weisz. Harry Houdini was merely a stage name developed later on. However, in order to eliminate confusion in this book, we will refer to him as Harry Houdini throughout.

Houdini was born in Budapest, Hungary, but moved with his family to the United States in 1878 when he was only four years old. It remains unclear what exactly precipitated this move, but Harry's brother Theodore later claimed that his father had a falling out with a Hungarian nobleman and ended up killing him in a duel.

This was supposedly the reason for the sudden flight out of the country. Due to its sensational nature, historians have been quite skeptical of this account, but it was indeed part of the family legend.

At any rate—whatever the reason for their departure—the family ended up moving to Appleton, Wisconsin, where Mayer received a rabbinical position at a local synagogue. The family was modestly successful in Appleton, but more changes came for the family when Houdini's father decided to uproot them from Appleton for a move over to the big Wisconsin city of Milwaukee. Rabbi Mayer was indeed a bit restless, always looking for something bigger and better. Houdini, too, would pick up this restless streak, and it would form part of his personality for the rest of his life.

Chapter One

Early Life

"The greatest escape I ever made was when I left Appleton, Wisconsin."

—Harry Houdini

After moving to the Wisconsin metropolis of Milwaukee, times were hard for the Weisz family. They lived in what could only be termed abject poverty as this family of immigrants struggled to make their American dream a reality. Mayer worked a string of different small-time jobs, occasionally working special events or teaching. The work proved to be sporadic, though, and Houdini's father just couldn't seem to get a break. At one point, the family was so desperate that Houdini's mother Cecilia even requested help from a local charitable organization called the Hebrew Relief Society. This aid organization had been established in 1867 in Milwaukee as a charitable resource for Jewish immigrants, and now it provided the family with much-needed assistance.

At this time, little Harry also picked up a job as a newspaper boy, hawking fresh copies of the *Milwaukee Journal* on street corners. The Weisz family was just barely eking out an existence. Making matters even worse, tragedy would strike in the worst possible way when Houdini was just 11 years old. In 1885, his older brother Herman, who had been sick for some time, passed away from tuberculosis. This was the first brush with death that the young Houdini had, and it opened his eyes to the fragility of life.

It was also around this age that his father began to speak openly to Houdini about his money problems and how he feared what might happen to the family after he was gone. As heavy as it may seem, Mayer even made little Harry promise to look after his mother in the event that he was unable to do so. Thus, by the time he turned 12, Houdini was essentially taking on the responsibilities of an adult, and it was at this tender age that he decided to depart from the home in search of a more permanent, money-making gig to help his family.

Shortly after he took off, his mother received a postcard on which Houdini had scribbled the message, "I am going to Galveston, Texas, and will be home in about a year. Your truant son, Ehrich Weiss." Instead of ending up in Galveston, Texas, though, he actually found himself in Kansas City, Missouri. Houdini hadn't quite mastered deciphering train routes and had gotten on the wrong train; instead of going south, he went west. Nevertheless, he tried his best to make do. In Kansas City, the boy set to work doing whatever odd jobs he could find, even resorting to shining the shoes of strangers if it could earn him a little money.

Houdini's father had in the meantime departed for New York in the hopes that he could find better-paying jobs in the Big Apple. In the midst of all of his cross-country train hopping, Houdini eventually found himself there as well. Here, he and his father would live in a simple boarding house as Rabbi Weisz struggled to get on his feet. It was once the situation had stabilized a bit that the rest of the family would come join Houdini and his father.

The holidays were a particularly rough time for the family since they would see folks out celebrating while they remained threadbare. It was these bleak conditions during one holiday season in particular that led Houdini to a rather ingenious scheme. He was working as a messenger boy when he had the idea to put a funny little message in the hat that he wore. Scrawled in big letters, the message read, "Christmas is coming. Turkeys are fat. Please drop a quarter. In the Messenger Boy's hat." It was a simple enough bit of marketing—but it worked. By the time passers-by finished reading the message, they were laughing hard enough that they couldn't resist dropping a quarter or two in Houdini's hat.

Houdini cleaned up pretty well with this gimmick, and by the time the holidays arrived, he had a great idea. He hid the coins all over his person and marched right up to his mother. He then told her, "Shake me! I'm magic!" Always ready for some fun with her mischievous son, she did as she was asked, only to see coins falling like rain from Houdini.

During his downtime, when he wasn't struggling to make some extra money, Houdini kept busy with the things that made him happy in life. He enjoyed swimming, running, playing sports, and soon he had developed a new hobby—magic. Houdini learned such things as putting a coin or playing card in his hand and then making it look as if it disappeared right before an observer's eyes. These were some rather simple parlor tricks, but soon the eager Houdini would learn more—much more.

Around this time, he heard of a famed illusionist from France by the name of Jean Eugene Robert-Houdin. Robert-Houdin was able to pull off some amazing stunts; it's even said he could make orange trees appear to blossom with the wave of a hand. With tricks like these, Robert-Houdin became a hero of Harry's, and as you might have guessed, it was from Robert-Houdin that Harry would eventually take the name he made so famous—Houdini.

Chapter Two

Becoming Harry Houdini

"An old trick well done is far better than a new trick with no effect."

—Harry Houdini

As a teenager, Houdini picked up a job at a necktie factory. It was hard, manual labor, but it helped him bring home extra cash for his family. If he had any money left over, he was likely to spend it on books about magic and performance art. Still obsessed with Jean Eugene Robert-Houdin, he wanted to learn to do the same stunts that had made Robert-Houdin famous.

His siblings would later recall how Houdini would get up on top of the roof of the family's apartment to practice magic tricks. Determined to find a way for himself, he would constantly practice flipping a coin through his fingers, and once he was quick enough, this skill translated into other magical illusions. His fingers were so quick that he could make a coin look like it suddenly appeared out of thin air—or even out of someone else's ear. Houdini was learning these standard magic tricks so that he could build upon this foundation of magical illusion even further. His partner in many of these acts was his brother Theodore (by then simply called "Theo" or even by his more whimsical nickname "Dash").

As his ability as a budding illusionist grew, Houdini became increasingly disillusioned with his job at the necktie factory, and so, in 1891, at the age of 17, he decided to call it quits. His mother is said to have been quite taken aback by this decision and couldn't help but be skeptical of Houdini's prospects of earning a living through magic acts. She is said to have questioned the young man, "So—from this you should make a living, my son?"

That was precisely what Harry Houdini intended to do. After branding his and Theo's act the Brothers Houdini, this rag-tag group of budding illusionists began taking all of the local social clubs, pubs, and any other local hangout by storm.

It was just as he was starting his magic career in 1892 that Harry Houdini's life received a terrible blow—for that was the year that his father died. His father had developed a form of oral cancer, and he quickly succumbed to the disease. Rabbi Mayer had often spoken with Harry about how the young man might one day have to take care of his mother and siblings, and upon his death, this responsibility became a clear reality. Cecilia is even said to have cried out at her husband's death bed, "Weisz, Weisz, you've left me with your children! What have you done?"

Houdini knew that it was now on him to provide for his family. Without his father around, he would have to take care of his mother and essentially become a surrogate father for his younger siblings. He knew it was going to be hard, but he couldn't bear to let them down.

With this mission in mind, Harry and Theo began performing at regular magic gigs. One of their biggest gigs came about a year after their father's death when they managed to get a spot at the Columbian Exposition at the world's fair in Chicago. The world's fair was a big deal at the time and was meant to commemorate the 400th anniversary of Columbus' expedition to America.

Here, the young brothers rubbed shoulders with more experienced artists, and Houdini learned a lot from just being around them. One illusionist even showed Harry a neat trick of swallowing several needles and a thread only to spit them up with the thread neatly woven through the eyes of the needles. Since many people have a hard time threading a needle the normal way—with their fingers—-this was quite a feat to say the least.

It was shortly after his stint at the world's fair that Houdini got a gig as a solo performer at a dime museum. The so-called dime museums of the late 1800s were essentially low-budget, circus-style freak shows that showcased various performers engaged in attention-getting acts such as fire-eating, contortion, swallowing swords, and the like. Houdini's act at the time consisted primarily of sleight of hand. He would make cards and coins disappear and was also known to make a handkerchief suddenly emerge from the flame of a candle. Such a trick no doubt involved having the hanky neatly wadded up in between his fingers, and the drama of gesturing over the flame served as a great distraction so that no one saw how the handkerchief emerged from his hands.

Houdini had also perfected an act which he dubbed the "metamorphosis." In this act, he would tie his brother Theo with a rope, place him in a sack, and then lock him up in a trunk. Houdini would then close a curtain in front of the trunk, do some hocus pocus, such as clapping his hands a certain number of times or uttering special words and phrases, and after a moment, whip back the curtain to reveal that Theo had escaped.

The secret, of course, was that there was a special escape hatch on the trunk that could be opened from the inside, and while the curtain was closed and Houdini was getting everyone's attention with his flamboyant theatrics, Theo was freeing himself from his confines. Although not exactly magic in the supernatural sense, the fact that Theo was quick and agile enough to wiggle himself out of a bag and squirm out of rope was a talent in itself.

Shortly thereafter, however, Theo botched an act and found himself unable to escape. A frustrated Houdini now insisted that he be the escape artist and Theo the magician. From there on out, it was Harry Houdini who was being locked up and confined, scrambling to get out, while someone else worked as the showman, getting the audience's attention.

These performances didn't make much, but Houdini sought to max out the meager earnings through sheer volume. He would perform around the clock, sometimes doing as many as 20 performances a day at the dime museum so that he could take home about $12 a week. This was good money for a low-budget performer in the dime museum circuit. True to his word to his father, he used most of his earnings to take care of his family. It's said that he would keep about $2 for himself and give the rest to his mother so that she would have enough money to pay the bills and buy groceries.

In answer to his mother's previous questioning of his choice in career—yes, Harry Houdini was indeed managing to make a living from his exploits after all.

Chapter Three

Love and Marriage

"The secret of showmanship consists not of what you really do, but what the mystery-loving public thinks you do."

—Harry Houdini

By the year 1894, Harry Houdini and his brother Theo were becoming regular fixtures of the performance art scene. Around this time, they were regulars at Brooklyn's famed Coney Island, and it was here that Harry was supposedly given some advice that would stick with him for the rest of his life. Houdini had a thick East Coast accent, and his choice of words made his upbringing clear. While there was certainly nothing wrong with that, on this occasion, a local huckster in show business approached the youth to critique his approach. The man asked, "Harry, why do you say, 'Ladies and Gents, as youse can see I ain't got nothing up my sleeve?'"

The man was pointing out Houdini's local slang talk, saying things like "Gents" instead of "Gentleman" and "youse" instead of "you." The man convinced Harry that if he wanted to appeal to a wider audience, he had to lose the local vernacular and adopt a more polished and classy form of speech. From that day forward, Houdini did indeed clean up his presentations and would later claim that he never used the word "ain't" again.

Although this was certainly a pivotal moment in Houdini's career, it was not quite as pivotal as what occurred a short time later. In the spring of 1894, Harry ran into an 18-year-old girl by the name of Wilhelmina Beatrice Rahner, or as Harry would call her, "Bess." Bess was a fellow performer who sang songs with a group called the Floral Sisters. It seems a little unclear how exactly the two first met. Like many instances taken from Harry Houdini's early life, their meeting is shrouded in mystery and, even more frustrating, conflicting stories.

Harry's brother Theo later claimed that he knew Bess first and even dated her and that Harry met her through him. Houdini, however, insisted that he first met this future love of his life when he accidentally dropped part of his magical paraphernalia right on her lap as they shared a public streetcar together. Bess had yet another variation of how they came to meet, claiming that she was in attendance at one of his performances when Harry accidentally dumped water on her.

Whatever the case may be, once they met each other, Harry and Bess fell deeply in love. After a very brief courtship, they were duly wed on June 22, 1894. It remains unclear how they spent their honeymoon, but Bess later reflected that it was "cheap, but glorious." Still, not everyone was happy about the marriage of this young couple. Bess's mother, who was a staunch German Catholic, apparently did not approve of Bess being with someone of the Jewish faith. Fortunately, though, Harry Houdini's family home welcomed the young woman with open arms. Cecilia loved her new daughter-in-law and immediately treated her as one of the family.

Houdini found not only a soul mate in Bess but also a new partner on stage. One thing that proved highly beneficial for Houdini's routine was the fact that Bess had a petite physique. Her tiny frame made her perfect for many of the tricks that Houdini pulled off that required someone who could get in and out of tight spaces. Shortly after getting married, the two went on tour together and hit up a wide variety of venues. At one point, they went to a place called Huber's Palace Museum in New York City, where they became a real crowd-pleaser.

Houdini meanwhile also tried to branch out from being just another performer to being an actual teacher of the arts. He wrote his first book, a piece called *Mysterious Harry Houdini: Tricks Requiring no Practice or Special Apparatus*, in late 1894. This book appears to have been a promotional pamphlet and a guide for budding magicians all rolled up in one. Houdini would go on to write several more books during his life, including *The Right Way to Do Wrong*, *Miracle Mongers and Their Methods*, and *A Magician Among the Spirits*.

At any rate, Houdini and his new stage partner Bess were at this point doing as many as 14 performances a day, and while Houdini was having the time of his life, Bess wasn't always so thrilled. Low-budget venues and what amounted to little more than seedy, hole-in-the-wall bars quickly started to take their toll on her. She made it clear that her participation was voluntary, and if she didn't feel up to it, she would stay home.

Nevertheless, in 1895, she and her husband went on a small tour that took them to

Pennsylvania to perform for the Welsh Brothers Circus. Here, Bess was able to showcase her dancing and singing ability. Houdini also diversified his act by adding a puppet show, as well as a kind of slapstick comedy routine. Not everyone was thrilled with his act, and at one point, someone in the audience hurled a piece of raw meat at Houdini as he performed, which hit him right in the head. He would have to work with a busted eye for the next several weeks.

No matter what other kinds of acts Houdini and Bess may have been performing, they made it their trademark to always end with a rendition of the metamorphosis trick. They had managed to get this act down so well, and they did it so quickly, that the audience was always impressed by it. Whether it was Harry or Bess in the trunk, the audience was always amazed to see the participant escape after just a quick parting of the curtain. Houdini realized, however, that as neat as this trick was, he needed to up the ante a little and come up with a new attention-getting stunt.

It was around this time that Harry Houdini began to experiment with handcuffs and locks. He wanted to figure out how to pick any lock with minimal effort. Doing this, he discovered that the infallibility of the average set of handcuffs was in itself an illusion, as most of them could be easily unlocked with a bit of effort and knowledge. He found that most cuffs were made in a very similar fashion, and if you figured out how to wiggle yourself out of one—you could break out of just about any of them.

Houdini developed innovative techniques of busting out of cuffs, such as using a thin piece of metal in the locks or even simply tapping on them at certain angles, which caused the locking mechanism to pop open. The most useful trick he learned, though, was how to hide a key to the cuffs on his body in places that no one would ever expect, such as in his mouth. Houdini could slip a key under his tongue, get locked up, and then presto—suddenly he was free!

Regardless of the fact that he might cheat by hiding a key, the real incredible feat was the fact that he could contort himself in such a manner to successfully use that key in the first place. Few people could do such a thing in the cramped spots that Houdini was put into. The pressure alone would have been enough to cause most people to hyperventilate, but Houdini learned how to calmly do what needed to be done in order to get out of these trying situations.

Another skill that he learned around this time was not for the squeamish; he mastered the art of swallowing whole objects and then regurgitating them back up on command. At first, he would practice this fine art with a small potato. The potato was a good practice object since if he failed to bring it back up, it would do no harm to his body. It was once he could bring up a potato on command that Houdini started swallowing other, less digestible, objects.

With this art mastered, he didn't have to hide the key to his handcuffs in his mouth—he could simply hide it in his stomach. No one would have ever guessed that Houdini was capable of such a thing, and it would remain a trade secret of his act as an escape artist.

Chapter Four

Fake Cures and a Healthy Dose of Scepticism

"I have made compacts with fourteen different persons that whichever of us died first would communicate with the other if it were possible, but I have never received a word."

—Harry Houdini

As time wore on, Houdini became more and more obsessed with his craft as a magician extraordinaire. He would practice routines for several hours on end, and according to his wife Bess, he was so focused on his acts that he often neglected things as basic as hygiene. She would later joke about how he would go to sleep in his clothes, wake up, and wear the same thing the next day.

Although Houdini was determined to succeed, sometimes sheer determination just wasn't enough, as he found out when he was arrested simply for performing. The incident occurred in a small Rhode Island community, which happened to have a law that prohibited performances on Sundays. It remains unclear if Houdini knew about the law ahead of time or not, but he and his whole crew ended up getting arrested by the police and thrown in jail.

Houdini, who often embellished many instances in his life, would later claim that he picked the lock in the middle of the night and set everyone free. This seems doubtful since, in the real world, the police take prison breaks quite seriously. If Houdini had really busted out of jail, they no doubt would have hunted him down afterward and arrested him again. Another more likely version of events tells us that it was the owner of the troupe who got them out simply by paying their bail.

At any rate, Houdini was able to bounce back from this disaster, and his performances were doing well enough that he was taking home around $25 a week, over double the $12 a week he had made when he was first starting out. It was enough money to help look after the rest of the family with some left over for Houdini to put into his savings. He also used some of his extra cash to buy part of the ownership of a burlesque traveling troupe called the American Gaiety Girls.

While Houdini tried to brand the show as "the finest, cleanest" burlesque extravaganza in the business, critics did not agree, and many of the performances were lambasted as being downright "vulgar." Nevertheless, Harry Houdini was a great promoter and could promote just about anything with enthusiasm and zeal. It was his great knack for promotion, coupled with his sheer talent as a performer, that would come together in his early recipe for success.

One of his greatest promotional gimmicks in these early days was to partner with none other than the police. Perhaps it was his stint in jail that gave him the idea, but Houdini developed a concept in which he would willingly turn himself in to the police and have them lock him up in several handcuffs before he attempted to escape. It was a great publicity stunt; people tend to take the police seriously, after all, so it certainly added to the drama of what Houdini was doing. The act was picked up by the local papers, and soon, there was a lot of chatter about this wild man named Harry Houdini.

Houdini now knew how to advertise and promote his exploits, and soon, he was coming up with even greater daredevil stunts to announce to the public. At one point, he began openly advertising that he would be placed, tied up, and shackled on the back of a crazed horse in Halifax, Nova Scotia. It sounded like a crazy enough event, and Houdini figured people would be sure to attend. They did, but the only trouble was that the horse was a little more crazy and unruly than he had anticipated. While he was contorting on its back to free himself, the horse suddenly bolted and took Houdini several miles away from the spectators. Houdini was indeed able to free himself after the horse came to a stop, but by then, the show was over.

Despite this mishap, Houdini had been doing well enough in his pursuit of greatness as a magician, but he and Bess were about to hit rock bottom. The group that had sponsored most of his acts, the so-called Marco Company, collapsed, leaving Harry Houdini suddenly without gigs. Now unemployed, Harry and Bess began to travel around the East Coast and Midwestern parts of the country seeking whatever work they could find. Houdini was for a time forced to change up his routine, and instead of just appearing as Harry

Houdini, he would do gigs as various personas such as "Professor Murat," the hypnotist, or "Cardo," the card shark. Bess in the meantime kept up her singing and dancing routine as always.

Houdini became so desperate that he sometimes resorted to gambling, an activity that would backfire on him big time in Chicago when he ended up owing $60. It might not seem like much now, but back then, it carried more weight—especially for a young couple like Harry and Bess who really needed it to get by. Nevertheless, they marched on, and soon they were taken to a place that Houdini did not expect to go: his old stomping grounds of Appleton, Wisconsin. Houdini had not been in his old hometown in well over a decade.

Everything went well enough on their impromptu tour of Appleton, but after everything was said and done, Houdini couldn't quite scrape together enough money to get back to New York. As such, during the holiday season of 1897, he and Bess ended up wintering down in St. Louis, Missouri, simply because they had no way to get home.

The couple was able to get a small one-bedroom apartment that winter but had no money for groceries. It's said that things were so bad that Houdini used his legendary quickness and agility to smuggle some potatoes out of a grocery store. It's certainly not something that his dear old mother in New York would have approved of, but Houdini had found himself in some really desperate conditions.

Many might have given up at this point, but Houdini wasn't ready to allow these temporary setbacks to get in the way of his dreams. He continued to pursue whatever gigs he could. Sometimes he was a magician, but other times he tried his hand as a comedian and did slapstick comedy. The biggest challenge for freelance performers like Harry Houdini was simply finding work.

Having that said, it was with great relief that he managed to enter into a deal with an entertainment company called Dr. Thomas Hill's California Concert Company in 1898. This was an old-school medicine show which traveled the country, starring Dr. Hill, a flamboyant showman who posed as a doctor and hawked phony cures while his crew of fellow entertainers performed for audiences. These exhibitions were usually conducted outside under tents or in the city on an open street corner.

For the performances, Houdini and Bess developed new personas. Harry began calling himself the "Great Wizard," and Bess who still sang her heart out was dubbed the "Little Vocalist." It was in this role that Houdini first got involved with paranormal fakery. At the behest of Dr. Hill, he expanded his act to include mindreading and poltergeist-type happenings such as making objects seem to move of their own accord and causing bells to ring without anyone being near them. This then eventually led to all-out stints of mediumship, in which the voices of the dead were supposedly heard. Such things were fairly popular in the late 1890s, and Houdini just played along with the popular sentiment.

It was perhaps due to his own efforts of faking such things that Harry Houdini would become a prominent skeptic of anyone who professed to speak to the dead.

Chapter Five

Houdini's Failed Attempts

"What the eyes see and the ears hear—the mind believes."

—Harry Houdini

After Dr. Hill's Medicine Show ran its course, Houdini and his wife were able to sign on once again with their previous traveling troupe, the Welsh Brothers Circus. Things began to look up for Houdini when the company allowed him to use his metamorphosis act as a main centerpiece for the entire circus. Every night, this act was used as the main event.

Being made a major attraction like this, Houdini wanted to look and feel at his best. This meant that he began working out to make himself more muscular and also engaged in plenty of endurance training by running, riding bicycles, and—when possible—exercising on the types of training bars that circus acrobats used. There was indeed a group of acrobats that performed at the Welsh Brothers Circus, so Houdini took advantage of their close proximity to work out on their equipment.

The then 24-year-old Houdini was known for his incredible energy, but as his time with the circus came to a close in the fall of 1898, he suddenly felt like he was running out of steam. Luckily, Harry and Bess were able to head back to New York to spend time with Houdini's family. Yet even during his downtime with the family, Houdini couldn't help but think about his next big gig, and he began advertising for it in advance. To his great disappointment, however, very few seemed interested, and he was forced to once again change his schtick.

This time, he put himself into the role of teacher and produced a special course called Harry Houdini's School of Magic. The scope of the course was grandiose, with Houdini promising to "sell his secrets" to anyone willing to pay for them. He didn't get very many buyers. Fed up, by the time the new year of 1899 rolled around, Harry was openly talking about giving up his dreams of being a performer. He began looking at 1899 as a make-or-break year, deciding that if he did not make it big, he was going to give up the whole thing entirely. Little did he know that 1899 would indeed be his year to succeed, and it was actually in the very first week of the new year that he got a big break.

Houdini had launched another great publicity stunt in Chicago by getting the police to create a public spectacle by slapping handcuffs and leg irons on him and then watching him attempt to escape before an enthralled audience. This was hyped up to be a major event ahead of time since his manager had chatted up all the local papers to make sure that there would be some journalists on hand.

It was a Chicago Police lieutenant by the name of Andrew Rohan who would be responsible for locking Houdini up. Houdini went to visit Rohan's precinct, and while his wife spoke with the officer, Houdini was busy staring at cell doors and prison bars. Just from a mere glance, he was able to ascertain all he needed to know. This no-nonsense cop proceeded to slap the cuffs on Houdini and also put him behind bars for good measure. Right there in front of the local press, Houdini was able to get out of the cuffs and force the prison doors open, walking out of the cell under his own power.

As great as this act was, some of the reporters expressed doubts, stating that it was likely that he had hidden a key on his person. This charge infuriated Houdini, who answered by pledging to do the whole thing again, except this time he would let himself get strip-searched to make sure that there were no keys on him. A drastic step for sure, but Houdini thought it was the only way to shut his skeptics up.

After everyone was assured that he had no keys, Houdini was cuffed and locked up again. This time around, he managed to free himself again, except he did so at a much more rapid pace than during the last performance. The event was received so enthusiastically that it ended up appearing on the front page of the *Chicago Journal*. Houdini was enraptured at the publicity, and after the papers hit the press, he exclaimed to his wife, "Bess—we've made it! I'm famous!"

It wasn't quite superstardom, but the publicity was enough to convince Houdini to keep going. Riding high on this acclaim in Chicago, he managed to get booked for some new gigs, but it was at one of these subsequent performances that Houdini finally would be met with a task he could not complete. A man in the audience at one of his performances came forward and dared Houdini to get out of a set of handcuffs that he had brought with him. Houdini was up for the challenge and allowed the man to bind him with the cuffs. He then took a moment behind a curtain, where he tried to struggle the cuffs off and even attempted to use a duplicate key. No matter what he tried, it didn't work.

In the end, it turned out that this failure wasn't quite Houdini's fault. The man—who happened to be a police officer—was good enough to explain to Houdini that the cuffs had been damaged, and the lock mechanism was broken. The officer then explained that the only way those cuffs could be taken off would be if they were sawed off. Houdini did not take to this prank too kindly. He learned a valuable lesson that day—to be careful when using someone else's props.

From that day forward, Harry Houdini would only use equipment that he knew was fully functional. He had made a mistake that fateful day in Chicago by agreeing to use faulty equipment, but he would not make that mistake again.

Chapter Six

European Tour

"No performer should attempt to bite off red-hot iron unless he has a good set of teeth."

—Harry Houdini

As Harry Houdini began to become more famous, he figured that the popular vaudeville circuit was most likely the best place for him to take his stardom to the next level. Shortly after his stint in Chicago, Houdini had gone off to St. Paul, Minnesota, and found just the kind of opening he needed. It was in St. Paul that one of his gigs was attended by a Vaudeville organizer by the name of Martin Beck. Mr. Beck was initially skeptical that Houdini was using real cuffs in his act, and so he presented a challenge to him. He told Houdini that he would buy three sets of brand-new ones and see if he could get out.

The officer who had tricked him into putting on broken cuffs was of course fresh in Houdini's mind, but Mr. Beck was offering to buy brand new, fully functioning handcuffs. Knowing that this equipment should be good, the escape artist accepted. The gambit paid off since Houdini was able to easily get out of them, and the man was subsequently impressed enough to offer him a job on the Vaudeville circuit.

Houdini was now traveling far and wide, wowing audiences all over with his daring feats as an escape artist. His pay had improved too—by now, he was regularly earning around $90 a week. Houdini once again sharpened his sense of advertising, sending out big, bold advertisements of his exploits in all of the local papers. As his acclaim grew, so did his paycheck. Soon, his $90 a week was bumped up to $125. It goes without saying that this was a lot of money to be made in those days.

By the year 1900, this Vaudeville notoriety would lead Houdini to even bigger and better things, as it was arranged for the now 26-year-old artist to leave the American circuit entirely in favor of a tour of Europe. Despite his previous success, making a European tour was a bit of a risk. No one knew for sure how well his acts that were so popular in America would play out in Europe. Nevertheless, Houdini had to try.

And so, on May 30, 1900, he and his wife Bess boarded a boat called the SS *Kensington* and traveled across the Atlantic to the first leg of their tour, which took place in Great Britain. Upon their arrival, the couple was put up in a boarding house in the bustling British metropolis of London. Once they were settled in, Houdini hit the ground running. He was soon booked at the Alhambra Theatre, one of the more famous Vaudeville joints in London. Here, he performed his escape acts, along with old classic stunts, such as his sleight of hand gimmicks and of course his metamorphosis routine. The performances were a success and brought him even larger attention from an unlikely source—Scotland Yard, the nerve center of British policing.

The idea was floated to Houdini that he should try to escape from handcuffs slapped on him by a group of policemen from Scotland Yard. Fortunately for Houdini, he had done his homework on British cuffs and was thoroughly confident that he had what it took to get out of them. After he agreed to the challenge, Houdini was slapped with a standard regulation issue, British police handcuffs. Making short work of these cuffs, all Houdini had to do to open them was tap them on one particular spot against a solid surface, and they would come undone.

Another famous stunt occurred shortly thereafter when he was taken straight to the headquarters of Scotland Yard and cuffed to a pillar right there in the hall. The policemen joked that they would allow him to hang out where he was as they returned to their office. They had barely turned around to leave before they heard Harry Houdini gleefully reply, "If you're going back to the office. I'll go with you." These hardened British detectives then turned around to see Houdini already free of the cuffs.

Houdini was now officially a sensation in London, and all of the local papers sung his praise. He was beloved by British audiences as much for his sense of theatrics as he was for his actual escapes. The artist was always sure to make each event an affair to remember. After his tour dates in England were through, Houdini then hopped over the English Channel and made his way to Dresden, Germany.

It was an interesting moment for Houdini to perform in front of an audience who spoke his native German tongue (although Houdini was born in Hungary and spoke Hungarian, he had grown up speaking primarily German). The

Germans were excited as well to have a German-speaking celebrity in their midst. Houdini himself later fondly remembered, "I had never addressed an audience in German before. I must have said some of the most awful things to make them believe I was good."

Houdini wowed the German crowd by agreeing to escape from cuffs and leg irons sent directly from a German jail. It's said that some of these contraptions were pretty heavy, weighing as much as 40 pounds (18 kilograms). All of his events were sold out for the rest of his engagements in Germany.

One of Houdini's greatest feats while in Germany was to have the famed Krupp armament factory specifically design the cuffs and leg irons to hold Houdini bound. Krupp designed manacles they felt Houdini would not be able to escape from, yet after the curtains went down in front of the escape artist, he sprang forth free from his bonds. The audience absolutely loved it. Houdini had raised the roof, and their cheers could be heard reverberating from the rafters.

Still, he paid a heavy price. "The cuff used was a kind of an arrangement that screwed to fit the hand," Houdini wrote to a friend shortly after the show. "And the Krupp man screwed it down until it touched the bone, and imagine the pain it caused me. The Krupp man has maimed my right hand so that I am unable to work, and it will be a week or so before I can have a cuff locked on me."

Houdini would sustain many more injuries like this during his career, and his hands and wrists were full of scars from failed and successful escape attempts.

Chapter Seven

The Prison Break

"It is not unusual for the eye or ear to play tricks with one, but when such illusions and delusions are taken for spirit forms of the departed and voices of the dead instead of being recognized as some subjective phenomena brought about by a physical cause, the situation takes on a grave aspect."

—Harry Houdini

Houdini finally wrapped up his extended tour of Europe in 1904, returning to the United States that year. Upon his return, he spent some $25,000 on a house in Harlem, New York. This was a home in which he intended for his mother to spend her final years as a fulfillment of his promise to his father to take care of her.

The home would also become a shrine to Houdini's career, with its shelves holding all the great souvenirs from Houdini's many journeys across the world as an escape artist. They also housed his books. Houdini was always a bit sensitive to the fact that he didn't have much of a formal education seeing as he had quit school to work at a young age. He tried to make up for this fact by being as well-read as possible, and his bookcase at this new home in Harlem paid testament to that fact.

Here, Houdini began collecting books on all manner of subjects, some of them actually quite rare. He owned, for example, a Bible autographed by Martin Luther. Considering the fact that even back then, such a tome was centuries-old, it was indeed impressive. Still, Houdini's most treasured artifacts were playbills from shows performed by none other than his chosen namesake: Robert-Houdin. Ironically, Houdini would write *The Unmasking of Robert-Houdin* only a few years later, in which he called out his former idol for being a liar and a fraud.

At any rate, although Harry Houdini enjoyed his new home in Harlem, it wasn't long before he was ready to take the stage once again. This time, he knew that he needed some fresh material. His new acts, which he would debut right there in the United States, would employ more dangerous conditions, such as feats that required him to hold his breath or be placed in pitch-black, tight spots underground.

In order to master the art of holding his breath, Houdini practiced by making use of a huge tub he had put inside his home. This thing would be filled with water, and Houdini would condition himself to stay under for longer and longer periods of time. He also regularly submerged himself in freezing water so that he would be accustomed to being in near-ice conditions. Coupled with this, he continued his typical routine of endurance-building exercises such as running and bicycling.

One of the most famous escapes that Houdini would involve himself in after his return to America didn't involve being underwater but rather in the confined space of a small prison cell. It was in January of 1906 that Houdini took it upon himself to escape from a prison cell at a penitentiary in Washington, D.C. This wasn't just any prison cell—it was the former cell of the man who had killed President James Garfield. The cell was surrounded by solid brick and had a massive door, held in place by a formidable steel bar locked in place. People said that the only way for Houdini to get out of this one would be if he learned to walk through walls. For some, that's exactly what Houdini appeared to do.

As was typical for all of his escape routines, Houdini was strip-searched beforehand, and it was made sure he wasn't hiding anything on his person. He was then placed in the cell, and to the shock of all, he was able to break out less than twenty minutes later. But that's not all he did—he had also opened up the other prison cells and had the prisoners switch to different cells before locking them back in place.

When he went up to the warden to fill him in on the old switcheroo, he was shocked, and so was the press. Still, not all of Houdini's feats were this successful. Soon thereafter, in fact, Houdini would meet with near disaster. In a rather reaching exploit, he had himself chained, cuffed, and closed up inside an iron boiler. The boiler was sealed up by bolts that were clamped down into it. In order for the trick to work, Houdini had a bolt cutter hidden on his person, and he was going to stun the crowd by cutting the bolts and then pushing them out before he himself hopped out.

In the middle of this exercise, Houdini had a problem. He cut the bolts, but their remnants were stuck in place, and after breaking off the ends of the bolts, the bolts got stuck. Houdini wasn't done yet, however, because as he struggled to get the bolts out, an idea came to him. He was able to take the bolt cutter apart and use it as an improvised spike and hammer, and with it, he slowly drove the bolts out.

It was still hard and excruciating work from the confines of that boiler, and in all, it took Houdini nearly an hour to get himself out of there. The audience was by then deeply concerned. They were all immensely relieved to see a clearly shaken but still very much alive Harry Houdini hop out to greet them.

Chapter Eight

Pushing Himself to the Limit

"I always have on my mind the thought that next year I must do something greater—something more wonderful."

—Harry Houdini

As the years went by, Houdini's feats became more and more dramatic. Since death was always a part of his stunts in some shape or form, it was only fitting that escaping from coffins became a big part of his routine. He also escaped from things that were much more peculiar, such as a giant leather football. Some of his exploits were even quite painful to experience. On one occasion in Toledo, Ohio, he allowed himself to be tied up and smeared with tar. It took him nearly an hour to free himself from this slippery mess, and Houdini later remarked that it was as painful as "hell."

In the years between 1906 and 1908, Houdini was particularly active. He staged dramatic dives into cold rivers, canals, and the like, tied up, handcuffed, and otherwise constrained. One of his most famous stunts during this period was a jump into the Mississippi River, which was witnessed by over 10,000 people. Another memorable instance was when Houdini submerged himself into the San Francisco Bay, with his hands cuffed and a 75-pound (35-kilogram) ball and chain attached to his leg. Although he succeeded in freeing himself, Houdini was frightened by this particular stunt since if he had erred even in the slightest, he knew that ball and chain would have sunk him to the seafloor.

Houdini knew the risks involved in some of these more dangerous stunts, and on one occasion before a particularly dangerous maneuver, he left a note to an associate, telling him to make sure that all of his money should be handed over to his wife should he perish. By now, Houdini had learned to make the potential risk to his life one of the more enticing draws of his overall performance. For example, he developed a trick called the Milk Can Escape, in which he would have himself placed in a large milk can and have it filled with water. The can would then be sealed shut, and the hand-cuffed Houdini inside would try to escape. Another version of this stunt saw Houdini shackled upside down and lowered headfirst into a tank of water, requiring him to hold his breath for more than three minutes while he freed himself.

Before going in, Houdini illustrated the danger by informing the crowd that should anything happen, his stagehands would bust open the milk can so that they could "do everything possible" to prevent his death. This was a reassurance that his act was not a suicidal one, and he intended to live, yet at the same time, the mere utterance of such a statement raised the specter of death. It was the suspense of it all that was irresistible to the crowds who flocked to see Houdini's exploits.

Houdini decided to take another tour of Europe in the meantime, and on August 10, 1908, he and his wife once again crossed the Atlantic. Upon his arrival, Houdini engaged in a whirlwind tour of Great Britain, France, Germany, and many other places in between. His feats became more elaborate, with Houdini deciding to ditch the curtain and perform most of them right before his audiences' eyes. Excited fans now got to see

Houdini as he struggled to break loose of whatever had him bound.

One of his most astonishing stunts during this tour occurred on July 1, 1909, in Scotland, when he jumped into Aberdeen Harbor during a terrible storm. The waves were so choppy that veteran mariners left the water, yet there was Houdini, ready to go in. He was wrapped in a steel chain and dumped off the deck of a tugboat. Houdini went down into the depths, but incredibly enough, he emerged in less than 30 seconds, completely free of his chains.

It was during this time that Houdini also developed an interest in airplanes and managed to buy a French Voisin Biplane for $5,000. He practiced flying the beast, and on November 26, 1909, he piloted it all on his own over the skies of Hamburg, Germany. In 1910, he then went to Australia by boat, with his plane stowed away on board, and repeated the feat there, becoming one of the first to fly a powered aircraft in the country.

Although he also did his usual escape artist stunts down under, he had a particularly hard time in Sydney. For one stunt, he was shackled and jumped 31 feet (10 meters) into the Woolloomooloo Bay but messed up and hit the waters face first. Although he survived the ordeal, the water smacking into his head gave him a couple of black eyes and loosened several teeth. The problem with Houdini's fame was that the more incredible his performances became, the more he had to top the last spectacular feat. Even if he didn't die in his exploits, the strain was starting to show on his form. Bess for one began to seriously fear that her husband was working himself to death.

Chapter Nine

A Tragic End

"Look at this life—all mystery and magic."

—Harry Houdini

In the fall of 1911, Houdini returned to America. Here, he performed many old favorites such as the Milk Can Escape and the like. As usual, though, he had to come up with something new and attention-getting. One of those attention-getting acts took place in Detroit, Michigan, where he had himself sealed inside a big sack. He was able to bust his way out with some effort, but afterward, he appeared to have injured himself. It was later discovered that a blood vessel had burst in his kidney from the strain. Houdini took it easy for a few weeks, but it wasn't long before he was back on stage doing it all over again, despite his doctor's warning that "by continuing your present regimen, you would be committing suicide."

Houdini toured heavily back and forth between America and Europe for much the rest of the decade, without much let-up. His mother had passed away in 1913. Her death was hard for Houdini to take and opened his mind up to the possibilities of the spiritual world. Although Houdini was a confessed spiritualist faker, he began to wonder if communication with the departed was indeed possible.

World War I then erupted the following year, effectively marooning Houdini in the United States since Europe would be a complete warzone until the war's end in 1918. Houdini in the meantime reprised his roles and engaged in more daring stunts. One of the most stunning from this period was one in which he was buried alive. The first time he performed this stunt, it nearly cost him his life. In this instance, Houdini was buried six feet (two meters) underground with no casket and had to claw his way through the soil using his hands. When he finally broke the surface, he was so exhausted and oxygen-deprived that he fell unconscious and had to be pulled out by his assistants. He later noted that the stunt was "very dangerous" and that "the weight of the earth is killing." In later versions of this stunt, Houdini had learned his lesson and was sure to use a casket.

After World War I came to a close in 1918, Houdini found a brand-new venue to use to engage a larger audience—namely, motion pictures. He signed on to do a 15-part series called *The Master Mystery*. The show was a suspense thriller in which Houdini played the part of one Quentin Locke. Quentin battled all kinds of villains during the series, including a giant robot named Automaton. The evil robot often bound Houdini in chains, prompting Houdini to have to free himself, thereby enabling him to showcase his classic escape artist talent on the big screen.

Houdini thought that he could become a real success in the movie business, bringing his stunts to a larger audience and at the same time reducing his workload. He only had to get his tricks on film, and then they could be repeated over and over for filmgoers without him having to lift a finger. It seemed like a great prospect to Houdini at the time, and soon, he signed an official contract with the movie company Players-Lasky for which he was paid $2,500 a week.

The first feature film that Houdini took part in was a piece called *The Grim Game*. This 1919 movie was another thriller that showcased his ability as an escape artist. *The Grim Game* was then followed by the films *Terror Island* (1920), *The Man from Beyond* (1921), and *Haldane of the Secret Service* (1923). The films were all fairly similar and got some rather negative reviews—not because of Houdini's stunts, but because of the silly plots involved. Nevertheless, Harry Houdini became a movie star in his own right and has his own star on the Hollywood Walk of Fame to prove it.

After he had his fill of the movie business, Houdini went back to reprise his live acts, but instead of doing escape stunts, he focused more on classic illusion acts. One of his most popular sleights of hand in his later years was a trick that made him look as if he could walk through walls. A solid brick wall was constructed on stage, and Houdini would walk behind a curtain on one side of the wall, only to immediately appear on the other side. Houdini accomplished this feat by actually wiggling under the wall, just as a trap door gave way, and then quickly getting to his feet on the other side. The fact that Houdini did all of this as quickly as he did is what created the illusion of him seamlessly walking right through the wall.

Harry Houdini had amassed an immense repertoire of stunts by this point in his career, but it was one of his oldest tricks that would end up killing him. Houdini was known the world over for being able to take a punch. He had perfected a means of tightening his stomach muscles so that if someone were to punch him, he would be unphased. In 1926, a fan tried to test him on this and asked if he could punch him in the stomach. Houdini told him he could but apparently wasn't quite ready for the blow.

The man suddenly began pummeling the artist's abdomen. Seeing that Houdini was distressed, his attendants demanded for the man to stop, but it was too late. Houdini became sick with terrible stomach pains and a high fever. Still, he went on to perform in two final shows before he passed out and was taken to the hospital. Here, doctors removed his appendix, and Houdini appeared to be getting better. A few days later, though, on October 31, 1926, Harry Houdini passed away at age 52. Apparently, his final words had been, "I'm tired of fighting... I do not want to fight anymore."

Conclusion

Harry Houdini was no doubt an incredible artist. He wowed the world with his feats of seemingly super-human ability. Yet as incredible as his exploits were, they weren't done with paranormal powers but rather painstaking training and practice. Houdini was the first to admit that he didn't have magical powers but rather sheer determination to find a way to come out on top.

Although interested in the potential of the supernatural, Houdini didn't put too much stock into it. In fact, he spent much of his career debunking the claims of mediums and spiritualists. Some of the more sensational conspiracy theories surrounding Houdini's death have alleged that perhaps the man who punched him backstage before his appendix ruptured was in league with the disgruntled mediums that Houdini had ridiculed. All of this is speculation, of course, and none of it is proven.

The mystery of Harry Houdini's abrupt and tragic demise only serves to add to the legend of—some would argue—the greatest showman who ever lived. There is indeed much about this man that still makes us all stop and wonder.

Bibliography

Begley, Adam (2020). *Houdini: The Elusive American.*

Houdini, Harry (1924). *Houdini: A Magician Among the Spirits.*

MacNab, Bruce (2012). *The Metamorphosis: The Apprenticeship of Harry Houdini.*

Posnanski, Joe (2019). *The Life and Afterlife of Harry Houdini.*

Savory, Tanya (2009). *The Amazing Harry Houdini.*

Sloman, Larry & Kalush, William (2006). *The Secret Life of Houdini: The Making of America's First Superhero.*

Sutherland, Tui (2002). *Who Was Harry Houdini?*

Printed in Great Britain
by Amazon

81287290R00037